The MAILBOX

The Education Center

Pick a Prompt

grades **K–1**

P9-DHA-582

77 reproducible writing activities

Every student page

✓ **Features a choice of three fun prompts**

✓ **Provides practice for different types of writing**
- explanations • narratives • stories • descriptions

✓ **Includes grade-appropriate writing lines**

✓ **Motivates students to write**

Managing Editor: Lynn Drolet

Editorial Team: Becky S. Andrews, Diane Badden, Kimberley Bruck, Karen A. Brudnak, Pam Crane, Chris Curry, Pierce Foster, Tazmen Hansen, Marsha Heim, Lori Z. Henry, Debra Liverman, Kitty Lowrance, Mark Rainey, Greg D. Rieves, Hope Rodgers-Medina, Rebecca Saunders, Donna K. Teal, Rachael Traylor, Sharon M. Tresino, Zane Williard

www.themailbox.com

©2012 The Mailbox® Books
All rights reserved.
ISBN 978-1-61276-155-8

Table of Contents

What's Inside 3

Fall

Start of school 4
Start of school 5
Apples 6
Apples 7
Constitution Day and Citizenship Day 8
Fire safety 9
Fall fun 10
Fall fun 11
Fall fun 12
Fall fun 13
Harvest 14
Harvest 15
Harvest 16
Halloween 17
Halloween 18
Thanksgiving 19
Thanksgiving 20
Thanksgiving 21

Spring

Spring fun 40
Spring fun 41
Spring fun 42
Spring fun 43
St. Patrick's Day 44
St. Patrick's Day 45
Spring babies 46
Spring babies 47
Earth Day 48
Gardening 49
Gardening 50
Flowers 51
Flowers 52
Butterflies 53
Picnic 54
Picnic 55
Beach 56
Beach 57

Winter

Winter fun 22
Winter fun 23
Winter fun 24
Winter fun 25
Winter fun 26
December celebrations 27
December celebrations 28
December celebrations 29
December celebrations 30
Polar animals 31
Polar animals 32
Martin Luther King Day 33
National Children's Dental Health Month 34
National Children's Dental Health Month 35
Groundhog Day 36
Presidents' Day 37
Valentine's Day 38
Valentine's Day 39

Anytime

Adventure 58
All about me...59
Amusement park......................................60
Books 61
Camping..62
Circus 63
Dinosaurs 64
Family...65
Farm 66
Friendship 67
Food 68
Habitat: desert 69
Habitat: pond 70
Habitat: ocean 71
Ice cream...72
Inventions 73
Neighborhood 74
Outer space 75
Pets 76
Royalty 77
Sports 78
Transportation 79
Zoo..80

What's Inside

77 student pages
231 writing prompts

Seasonal pages

So Many Pumpkins!

✂ Cut.
Glue.
✏ Write.

Name _____

| From Seed to Pumpkin | A Trip to the Pumpkin Patch | The Pumpkin That Would Not Stop Growing! |

Pick a Prompt • ©The Mailbox® Books • TEC61342

14

A Snowy Day

Name _____

✔ Check one.
✏ Write.

Winter fun

☐ I like cold weather because...
☐ Too Much Snow!
☐ Fun on the Ice

Pick a Prompt • ©The Mailbox® Books • TEC61342

Anytime pages

Lots of Books

Name _____

✔ Check one.
✏ Write.

Books

☐ My Favorite Book
☐ Reading is...
☐ Why do I like books?

Pick a Prompt • ©The Mailbox® Books • TEC61342

19

Special day pages

A Great Country

Name _____

✔ Check one.
✏ Write.

Constitution Day and Citizenship Day

☐ A New Law
☐ Why is it great to live in America?
☐ How to Be a Good Citizen

Pick a Prompt • ©The Mailbox® Books • TEC61342

8

Back-to-School

✂ Cut.

🫙 Glue.

✏ Write.

Welcome!

To get ready for a school day, I…	First-Day Feelings	The Best School Day Ever!

In the Classroom

✔ Check one.

☐ How to Have a Great School Day

☐ Learning Is Fun

☐ Whew, That Was Hard!

✏ Write.

Yummy Apples

✓ Check one.

✏ Write.

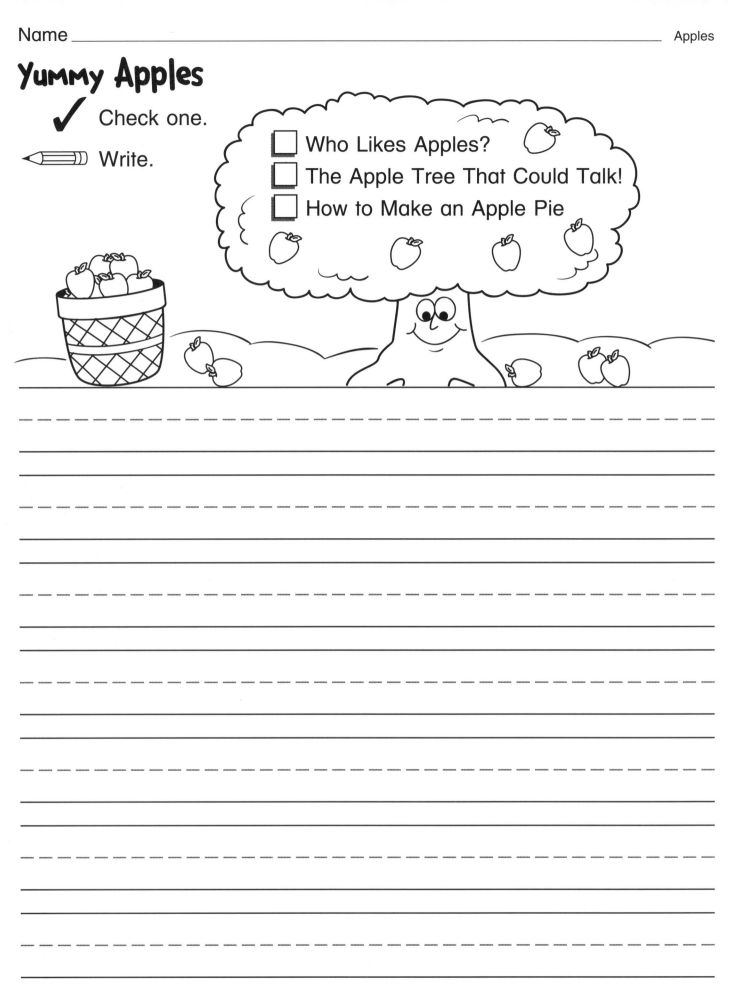

☐ Who Likes Apples?
☐ The Apple Tree That Could Talk!
☐ How to Make an Apple Pie

6   *Pick a Prompt* • ©The Mailbox® Books • TEC61342

Name

Apples on the Run

Cut.

Glue.

Write.

Pick a Prompt • ©The Mailbox® Books • TEC61342

Why are the apples running?

Boom!
The Apple That Fell Down!

A Silly Sunny Day

A Great Country

✓ Check one.

✏ Write.

☐ A New Law
☐ Why is it great to live in America?
☐ How to Be a Good Citizen

Thank You, Firefighters!

Cut.

Glue.

Write.

A firefighter is my friend because...

A Firefighter's Uniform

Fire Safety Dos and Don'ts

Happy Fall!

✓ Check one.

✏ Write.

☐ When the weather gets cooler, I like to....

☐ The Busy Squirrel

☐ There is a lot to see, hear, and smell in the fall!

It's Football Season

✂ Cut.

🍾 Glue.

✏ Write.

| The Big Game! | How to Be a Football Fan | Football is… |

Name _____

Lots of Leaves

✂ Cut.

🖌 Glue.

✏ Write.

- -

| Fun With Leaves | Who's there? | Mouse Gets Lost in the Leaves |

Name _____

A Fall Day

✓ Check one.

✏ Write.

☐ A Fall Hike

☐ Lion looks for....

☐ Why do I like fall?

So Many Pumpkins!

✂ Cut.

🔖 Glue.

✏ Write.

_____

_____

_____

_____

_____

_____

_____

_____

_____

_____

_____

_____

Pick a Prompt • ©The Mailbox® Books • TEC61342

| From Seed to Pumpkin | A Trip to the Pumpkin Patch | The Pumpkin That Would Not Stop Growing! |

Pumpkin Time

✔ Check one.

✏ Write.

☐	☐	☐
How to Make Pumpkin Pie	My pumpkin is…	Why the Littlest Pumpkin Won the Prize

_____

_____

_____

_____

_____

_____

_____

_____

_____

_____

_____

_____

Sleepy Scarecrow

✂ Cut.

🗴 Glue.

✏ Write.

Why the Scarecrow Is So Sleepy	The Crow and the Scarecrow	When the scarecrow fell asleep…

Jack-o'-Lantern Designs

✓ Check one.

✏ Write.

☐ How to Make a Jack-o'-Lantern

☐ A Very Proud Fox

☐ The Glowing Jack-o'-Lantern

Happy Halloween!

Cut.

Glue.

Write.

Trick
or
Treat

| My Favorite Treats | The Halloween Party | When I get dressed up, I... |

The Tapping Turkeys

✓ Check one.

✏ Write.

☐ What a
Show!

☐ The Farmer Looks
for His Turkeys

☐ If I could be
on stage, I...

_____

- -

_____

- -

_____

- -

_____

- -

_____

- -

_____

- -

_____

- -

_____

It's Turkey Day!

✓ Check one.

✏ Write.

☐ I am thankful for...

☐ Turkey's Big Mess!

☐ Friends Share a Meal

Name _____

Happy Thanksgiving!

✂️ Cut.

🗒️ Glue.

✏️ Write.

_____

_____

_____

_____

_____

_____

_____

Pick a Prompt • ©The Mailbox® Books • TEC61342

How the Indians Helped the Pilgrims	On Thanksgiving, I...	The Best Meal Ever!

Dressing for Winter

✓ Check one.

✏ Write.

☐ The Confused Pup!

☐ How to Dress for Cold Weather

☐ A Favorite Winter Outfit

Pick a Prompt • ©The Mailbox® Books • TEC61342

Comfy and Cozy

✂️ Cut.

🧴 Glue.

✏️ Write.

| How to Make Hot Cocoa | When it snows, I like to... | Elephant's Pajama Day |

Name _____

24

A Snowy Day

✓ Check one.

✏️ Write.

I like cold weather because…

☐ I like cold weather because…
☐ Too Much Snow!
☐ Fun on the Ice

Silly Snowpals

✂️ Cut.

🧴 Glue.

✏️ Write.

_____
_____
_____
_____
_____
_____
_____
_____
_____
_____
_____
_____

Pick a Prompt • ©The Mailbox® Books • TEC61342

| Silly Snowpals | If the snowpals came to life,… | How to Make a Snowpal |

26

Brrrr!

✓ Check one.

✏ Write.

☐ The Magical Snow Skis!

☐ Things to Do in the Winter

☐ When I get cold,....

Happy Holidays!

Cut.

Glue.

Write.

Pick a Prompt • ©The Mailbox® Books • TEC61342

Merry Christmas!

Happy Hanukkah!

Celebrate Kwanzaa!

At the North Pole

Cut.

Glue.

Write.

_____

- -
_____

- -
_____

- -
_____

- -
_____

- -
_____

- -
_____

- -
_____

Pick a Prompt • ©The Mailbox® Books • TEC61342

Pin the Nose on the Reindeer	I would like to tell Santa…	The Elf Who Saved the Day!

Name _____

Presents and Parties

✂ Cut.

△ Glue.

✏ Write.

Pick a Prompt • ©The Mailbox® Books • TEC61342

| The Best Present Ever! | My family likes to… | A Great Holiday Party |

29

Holiday Singers

✔ Check one.

✏ Write.

☐ Singing in the Snow

☐ The Fox That Would Not Sing

☐ Holiday music makes me feel...

Name _____

Look, a Polar Bear!

✓ Check one.

☐ A Playful Polar Bear

☐ Polar Bear's Funny Dive

☐ A polar bear looks like...

✏ Write.

_____
_____
_____
_____
_____
_____
_____
_____

Pick a Prompt • ©The Mailbox® Books • TEC61342

31

Slipping and Sliding

✂️ Cut.

🧴 Glue.

✏️ Write.

| A Great Day for Penguin | The Super Slider | Watch Out! |

Making a Difference

✓ Check one.

✏ Write.

☐ I think Martin Luther King Jr.....

☐ What Peace Means to Me

☐ What is your dream?

Martin Luther King Jr.

Name _____

Great Grin!

✂ Cut.

🧴 Glue.

✏ Write.

_____

- -

_____

- -

_____

- -

_____

- -

_____

- -

_____

- -

_____

Pick a Prompt • ©The Mailbox® Books • TEC61342

| How to Brush Your Teeth | A Visit to the Dentist | The Worst Toothache Ever! |

Take Care of Your Teeth

✓ Check one.

✏ Write.

☐ I Lost a Tooth!
☐ Floss, Brush, Rinse
☐ The Happy Tooth

Wake Up, Groundhog!

✂ Cut.

Glue.

✏ Write.

_____

- - - - - - - - - - - - - - - - - - - -

_____

- - - - - - - - - - - - - - - - - - - -

_____

- - - - - - - - - - - - - - - - - - - -

_____

- - - - - - - - - - - - - - - - - - - -

_____

- - - - - - - - - - - - - - - - - - - -

_____

- - - - - - - - - - - - - - - - - - - -

_____

Pick a Prompt • ©The Mailbox® Books • TEC61342

I Woke Up the Groundhog!	My Weather Prediction	If the groundhog sees its shadow, I will feel...

Name _____

Celebrate Leadership

✂ Cut.

📎 Glue.

✏ Write.

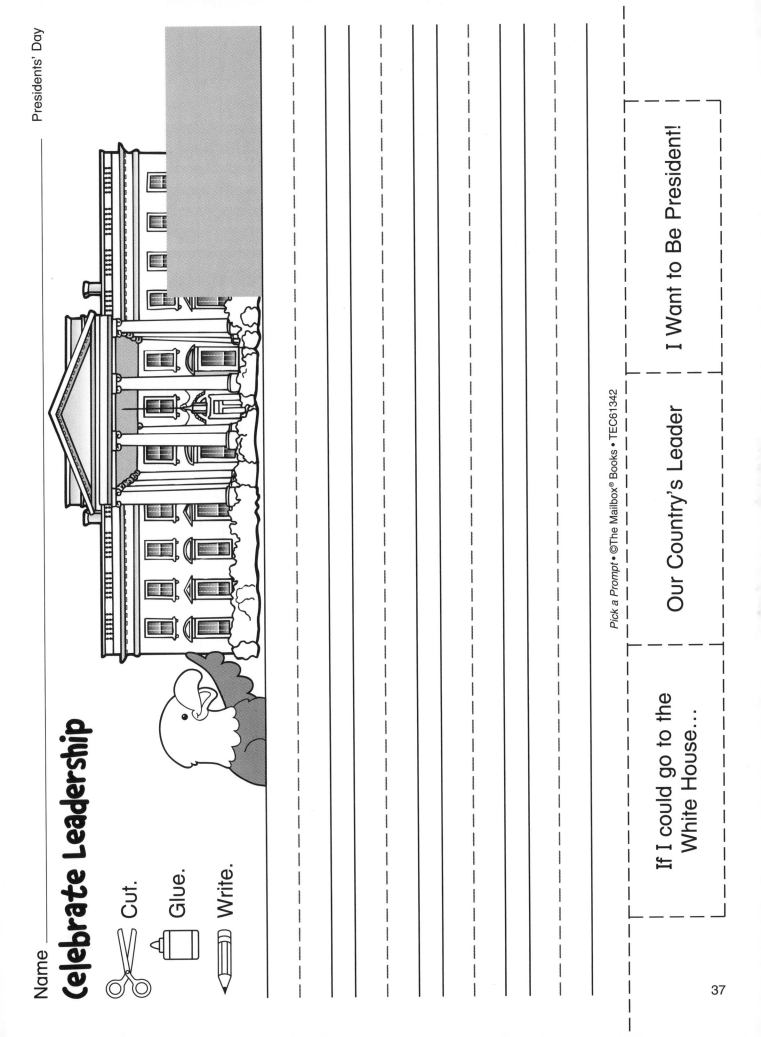

_ _

_ _

_ _

_ _

_ _

_ _

Pick a Prompt • ©The Mailbox® Books • TEC61342

| If I could go to the White House… | Our Country's Leader | I Want to Be President! |

37

Name

38

Happy Valentine's Day!

✓ Check one.

☐ A Fun Party!

☐ A best friend....

☐ How to Make a Card

✏ Write.

Someone Special

✂ Cut.

🖉 Glue.

✏ Write.

I love you!

_____
_ _
_____
_____
_ _
_____
_____
_ _
_____
_____
_ _
_____

Somebody Loves Me!	A Special Day	I love my…

Lamb's Kite

✂ Cut.

🧴 Glue.

✏ Write.

_____

_____

_____

_____

_____

_____

_____

_____

_____

_____

_____

_____

_____

_____

Pick a Prompt • ©The Mailbox® Books • TEC61342

| A Cool Kite! | How to Fly a Kite | Help for Lamb |

It's Raining!

✓ Check one.

✎ Write.

☐ When it rains, I like to....

☐ Stuck in the Mud!

☐ Ready for a Rainy Day

Whoosh!

✂ Cut.

🪣 Glue.

✏ Write.

| Oh, no! Bunny is… | When Bunny gets home,… | A New Umbrella |

Golf, Anyone?

✓ Check one.

✏ Write.

Lion Loses a Golf Ball!

Why do I like spring?

My Favorite Spring Sport

Hole 9

44 Name _____

Happy St. Patrick's Day!

✂ Cut.

▭ Glue.

✏ Write.

_____

_____

_____

_____

_____

_____

Pick a Prompt • ©The Mailbox® Books • TEC61342

The Happy Leprechaun

If I met a leprechaun,…

My Luckiest Day Ever!

Leprechaun's Bad Day

✓   Check one.

✏   Write.

☐ The Unlucky Leprechaun
☐ Who Took the Gold?
☐ My Bad Day

Keep Out!

_____
_____
_____
_____
_____
_____
_____
_____
_____
_____
_____
_____

Welcome, Chicks!

Cut.

Glue.

Write.

_____

- -

_____

_____

- -

_____

_____

- -

_____

_____

- -

_____

_____

- -

_____

Pick a Prompt • ©The Mailbox® Books • TEC61342

| After the chicks hatched,… | Proud Mama! | Baby Chick Finds a Friend |

Name _____

Hello, Ducks!

✓ Check one.

✏️ Write.

☐ A Big, Fluffy Family

☐ A Trip to the Pond

☐ Little Duck Gets Lost

Help Our Earth

✓ Check one.

✏ Write.

☐ Don't Litter!
☐ I can help the earth by...
☐ Cleanup Day

The Happy Gardener

✂ Cut.

🧴 Glue.

✏ Write.

| A Healthy Garden | The Surprise Plants | The Plant That Grew and Grew! |

50 Name _____

A Vegetable Garden

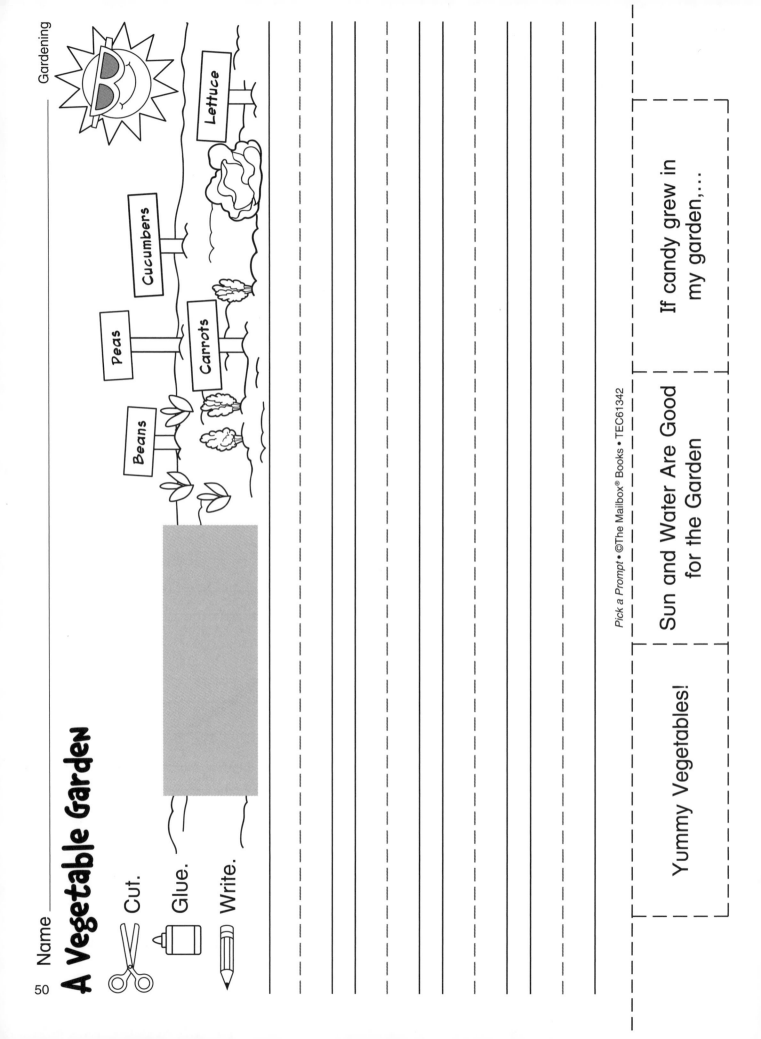

Cut.

Glue.

Write.

Pick a Prompt • ©The Mailbox® Books • TEC61342

| Yummy Vegetables! | Sun and Water Are Good for the Garden | If candy grew in my garden,... |

At the Flower Shop

✓ Check one.

✏ Write.

☐ The Really Big Flower!   ☐ I would get flowers for…

☐ The Case of the Missing Flowers

_____

- -

_____

- -

_____

- -

_____

- -

_____

- -

_____

- -

_____

- -

_____

Name _____

Healthy Flowers

✔ Check one.

✏ Write.

Flowers need…

☐ The Parts of a Flower

☐ The Ladybug Helps the Flower!

Name

Caterpillars and Butterflies

Cut.

Glue.

Write.

A Beautiful Butterfly!

Pick a Prompt • ©The Mailbox® Books • TEC61342

The Caterpillar That Wanted to Fly

First, there was an egg…

53

Food and Fun Outdoors

✓ Check one.

✏ Write.

☐ A Family Picnic   ☐ When I go on a picnic,....   ☐ The Puppies' Picnic

The Picnic Basket

✂ Cut.

△ Glue.

✎ Write.

_____
- - - - - - - - - - - - - - - - -
_____
- - - - - - - - - - - - - - - - -
_____
- - - - - - - - - - - - - - - - -
_____
- - - - - - - - - - - - - - - - -
_____
- - - - - - - - - - - - - - - - -
_____
- - - - - - - - - - - - - - - - -
_____

Pick a Prompt • ©The Mailbox® Books • TEC61342

| Who Left the Basket? | A Tasty Surprise | How to Pack for a Picnic |

Sandy Seashore

Cut.

Glue.

Write.

| Crab Builds a Sand Castle | Fun in the Sun! | How to Keep Cool |

Fun in the Water

✓ Check one.

✏️ Write.

☐ When I go to the beach,...
☐ Pelican Goes Surfing
☐ Animals in the Ocean

Name _____

The Magic Carpet Ride

✓ Check one.

✏️ Write.

☐ A Great Adventure!

☐ It Was Only a Dream

☐ At first the ride was bumpy…

Me, Me, Me!

✂ Cut.

🧴 Glue.

✏ Write.

Draw yourself!

_____

- -

_____

- -

_____

- -

_____

- -

_____

- -

_____

- -

_____

Pick a Prompt • ©The Mailbox® Books • TEC61342

My Favorite Food	I am special...	Things That Make Me Smile

At the Amusement Park

✓ Check one.

✏ Write.

☐ Wow, What a Ride!

☐ It was fun to…

☐ All Wet on the Water Ride

Name _____

Lots of Books

✓ Check one.

✏️ Write.

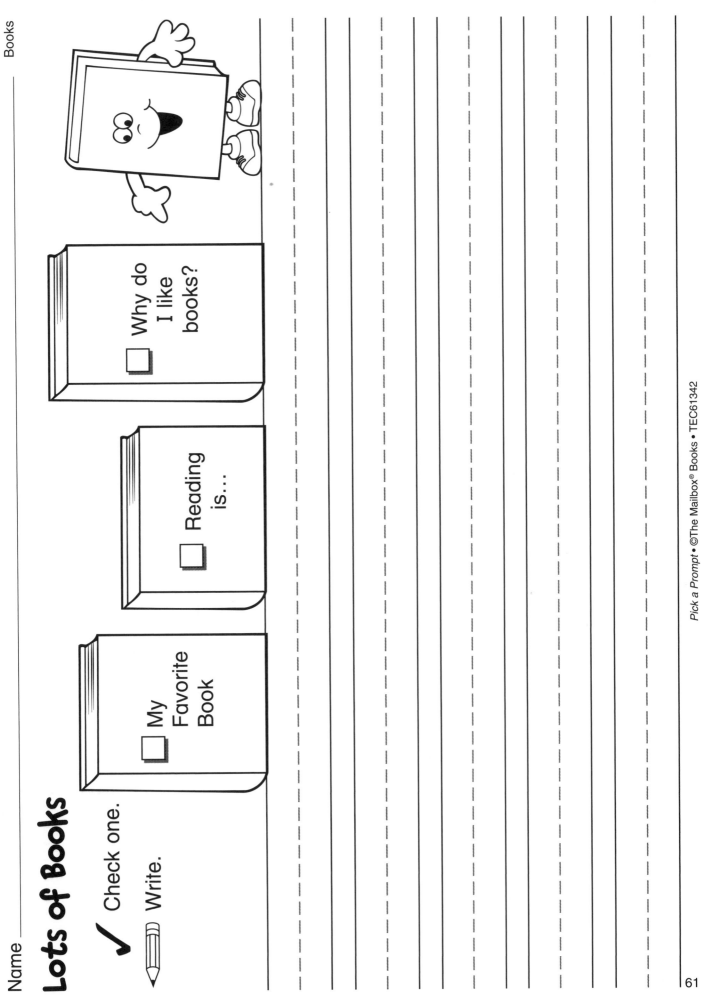

My Favorite Book

☐

Reading is...

☐

Why do I like books?

☐

Pick a Prompt • ©The Mailbox® Books • TEC61342

62 Name

Away From Home

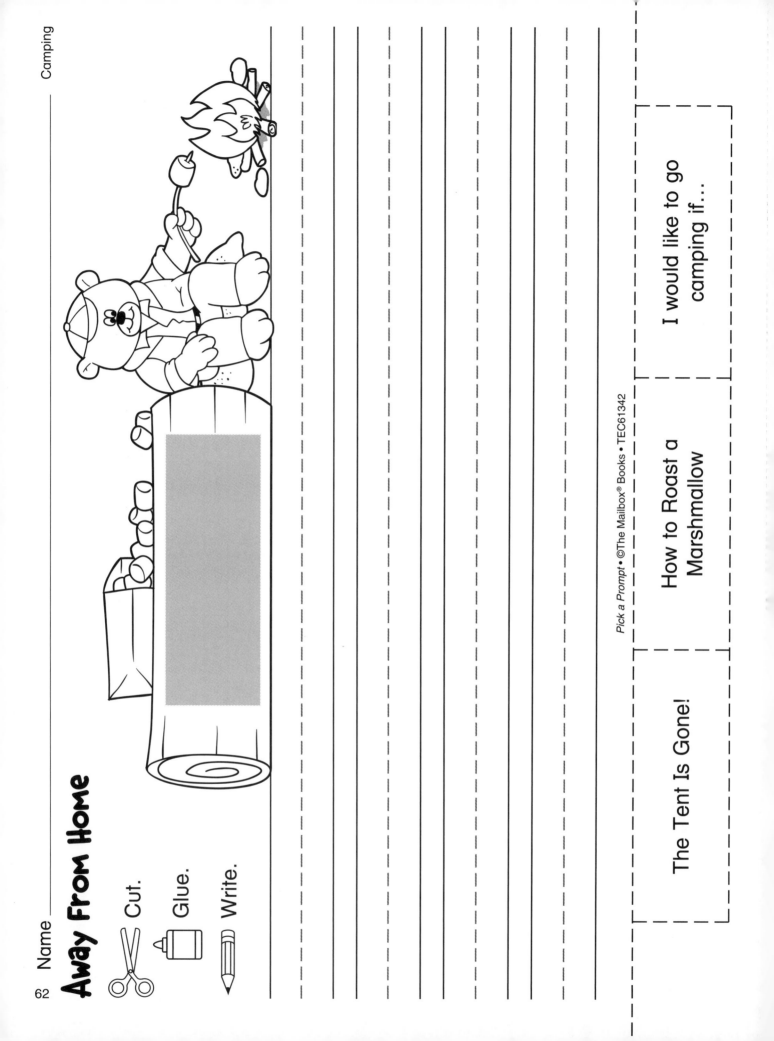

Cut.

Glue.

Write.

Pick a Prompt • ©The Mailbox® Books • TEC61342

| The Tent Is Gone! | How to Roast a Marshmallow | I would like to go camping if... |

The Circus Is Here!

✓ Check one.

✏ Write.

☐ The Amazing Circus Animals
☐ Circus Sights and Sounds
☐ The Funny Clown

Name _____

Baby Dinosaurs?

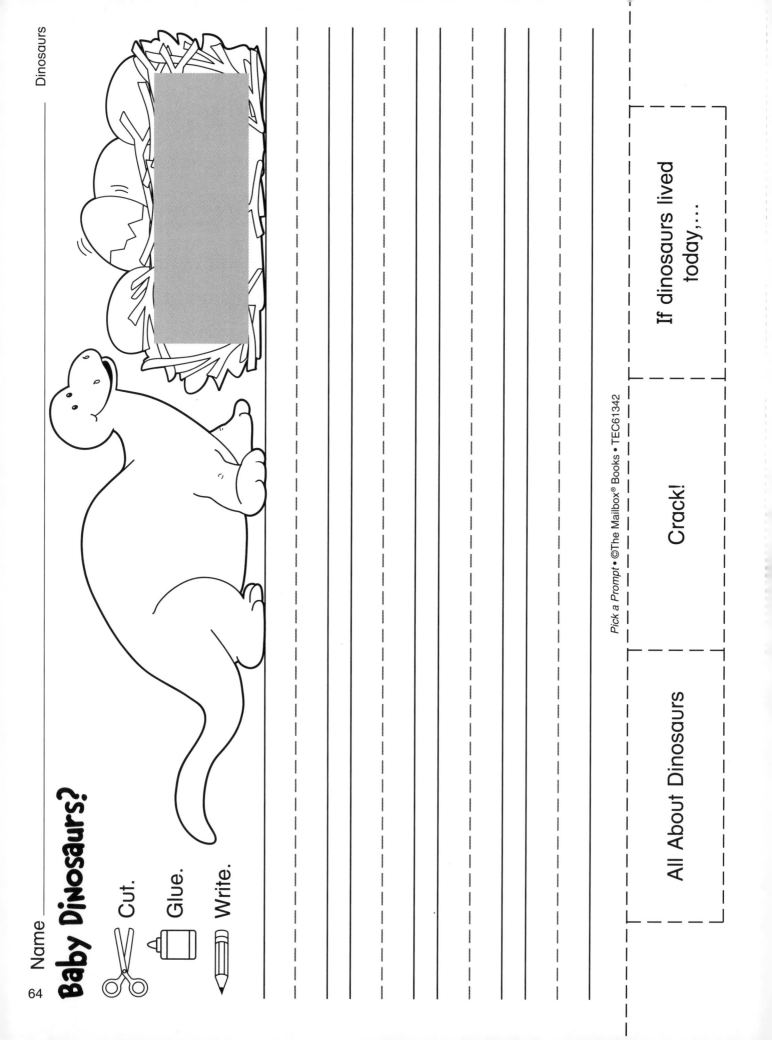

✂ Cut.

🗴 Glue.

✏ Write.

All About Dinosaurs

Crack!

If dinosaurs lived today,....

At Home

✂ Cut.

🗴 Glue.

✏ Write.

| I love my family because… | Pets Are Family Too! | Let me tell you about my family. |

On the Farm

✔ Check one.

✏ Write.

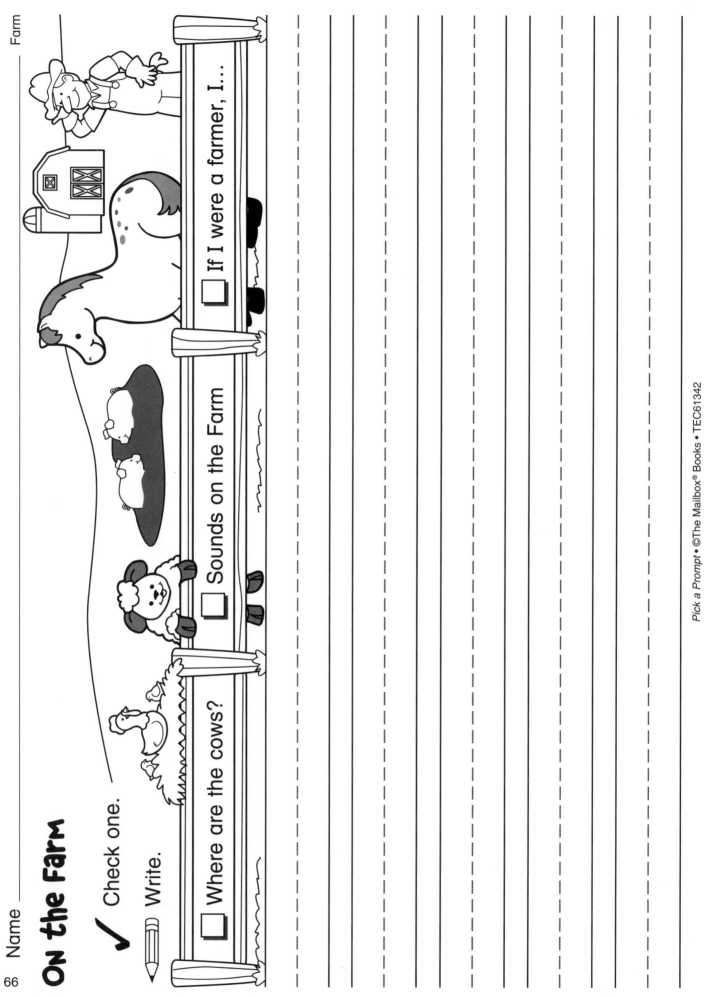

☐ Where are the cows?

☐ Sounds on the Farm

☐ If I were a farmer, I...

Name _____

Hello, Friend!

✂ Cut.

🖊 Glue.

✏ Write.

How to Be a Good Friend

All About My Friend

My friend and I like to...

I'm Hungry!

✂️ Cut.

Glue.

✏️ Write.

| My favorite food is… | How to Make a Pizza | The Dog Ate My Lunch! |

Habitat: desert

The Dry Desert

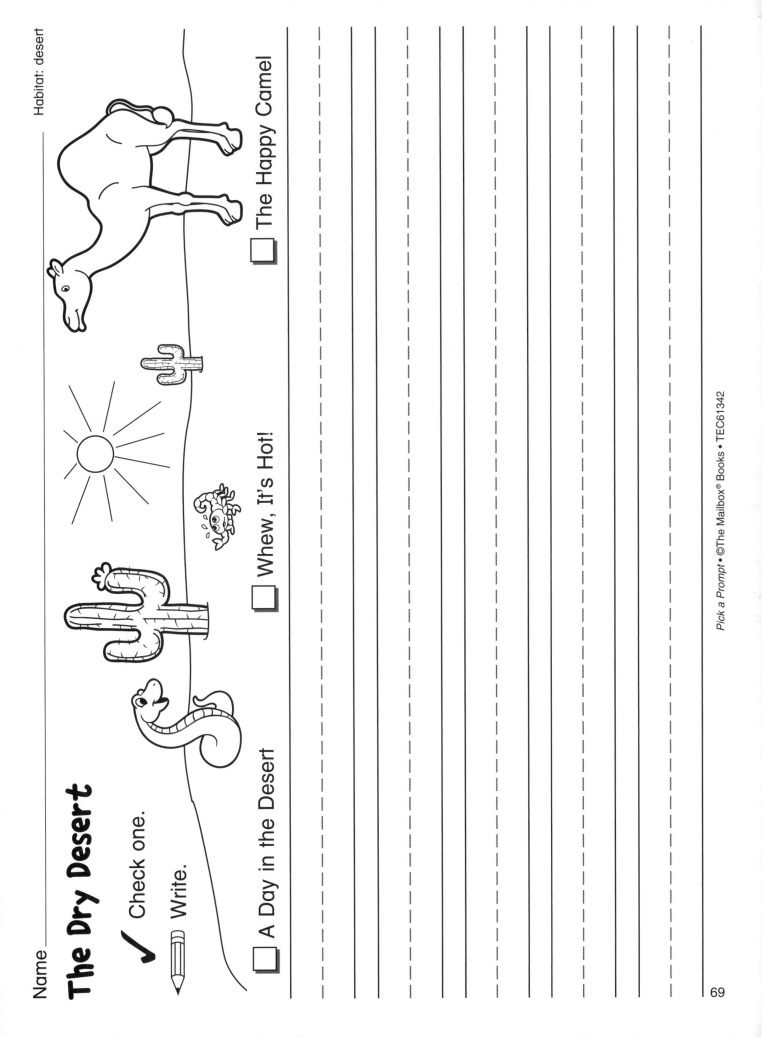

✓ Check one.

✏ Write.

☐ The Happy Camel

☐ Whew, It's Hot!

☐ A Day in the Desert

At the Pond

✓ Check one.

✏ Write.

- ☐ A Visit to the Pond
- ☐ Splash!
- ☐ What lives at the pond?

Name _____

Bottom of the Ocean

Cut. ✂

Glue. 🧴

Write. ✏

Habitat: ocean

Pick a Prompt • ©The Mailbox® Books • TEC61342

The Sunken Ship

If I could swim like a shark, I...

Wow, What a Sparkly Fish!

71

Who Wants Ice Cream?

✔ Check one.

✏ Write.

☐ The Very Best
Ice Cream Cone

☐ Why do I
like ice cream?

☐ Too Much
Ice Cream!

Something New!

✓ Check one.

✏ Write.

Plan

☐ Rat's New Ride!

☐ I am happy someone invented....

☐ My Idea for an Invention

A Very Strange Park

✂ Cut.

🧴 Glue.

✏ Write.

Hiccup!

Hiccup!

The Dancing Bush	When I went to the park,...	A Slide That Hiccups?

Way Out There!

✓ Check one.

✏ Write.

I see stars, planets,...

Fido

☐ My Pet Made It to the Moon!
☐ If I could ride in a spaceship...
☐ My Friend Is an Alien

_____

_____

_____

_____

_____

_____

_____

_____

_____

_____

_____

_____

_____

_____

Woof! Meow! Chirp!

Cut.

Glue.

Write.

| I like pets because… | I know what a veterinarian does. | How to Take Care of a New Pet |

A Great Story

✂ Cut.

Glue.

✏ Write.

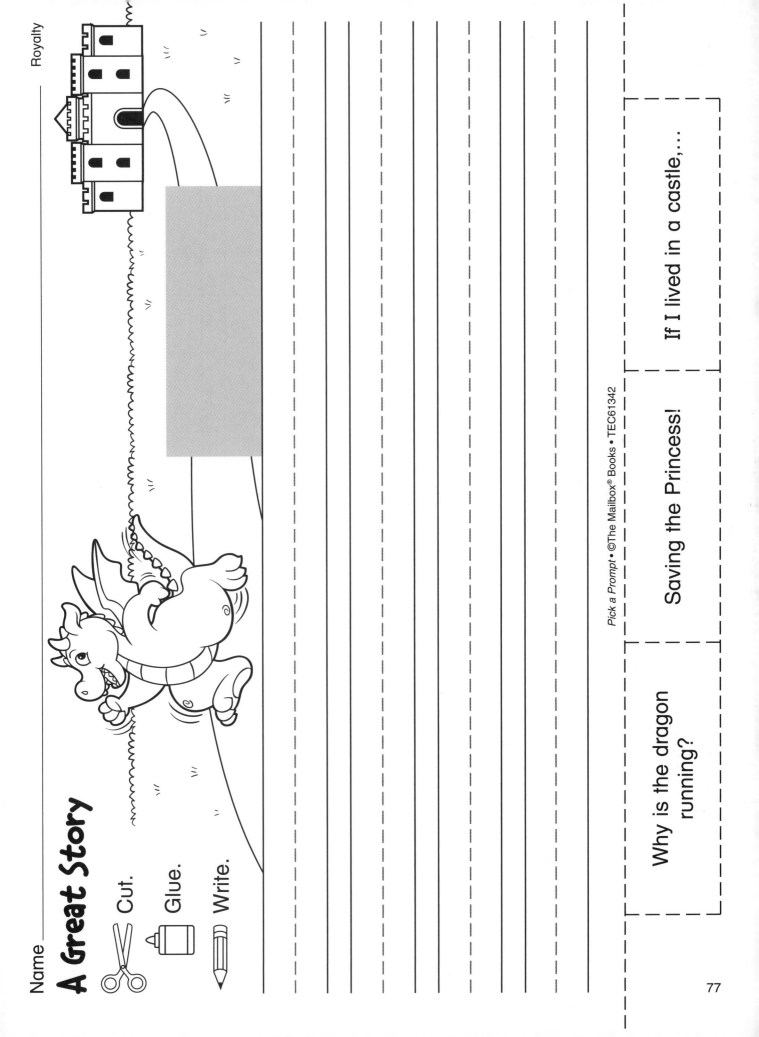

Pick a Prompt • ©The Mailbox® Books • TEC61342

Why is the dragon running?

Saving the Princess!

If I lived in a castle,....

78

All About Sports

Name _____

✓ Check one.

✏️ Write.

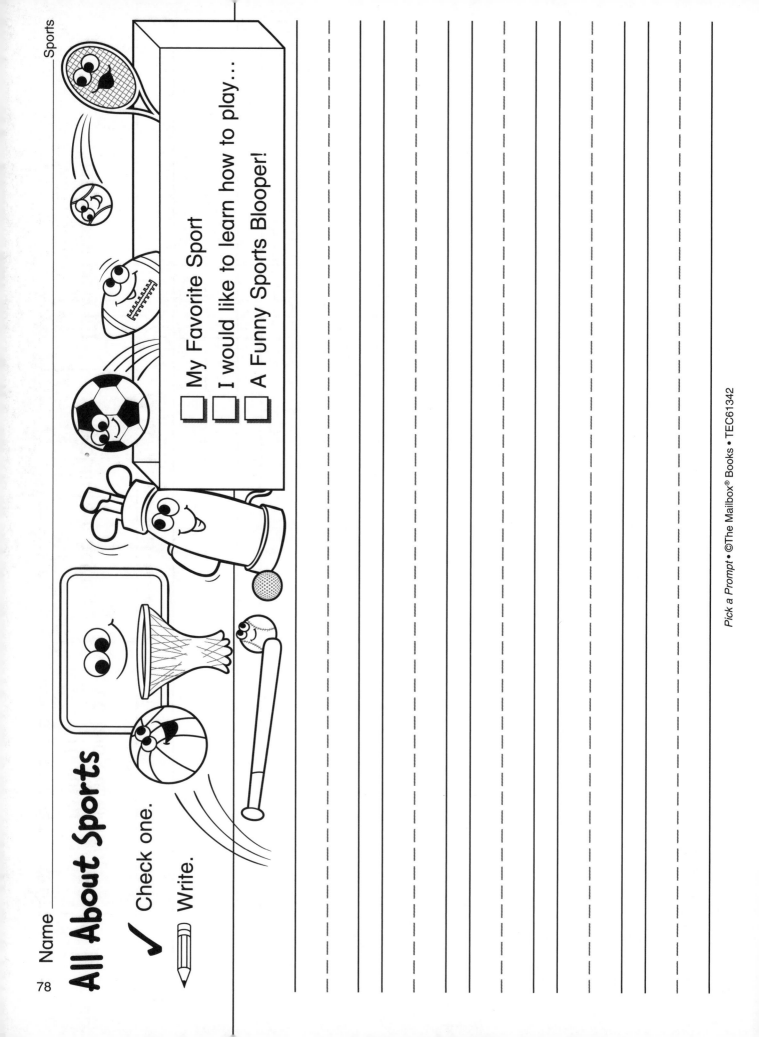

☐ My Favorite Sport

☐ I would like to learn how to play...

☐ A Funny Sports Blooper!

Ways to Travel

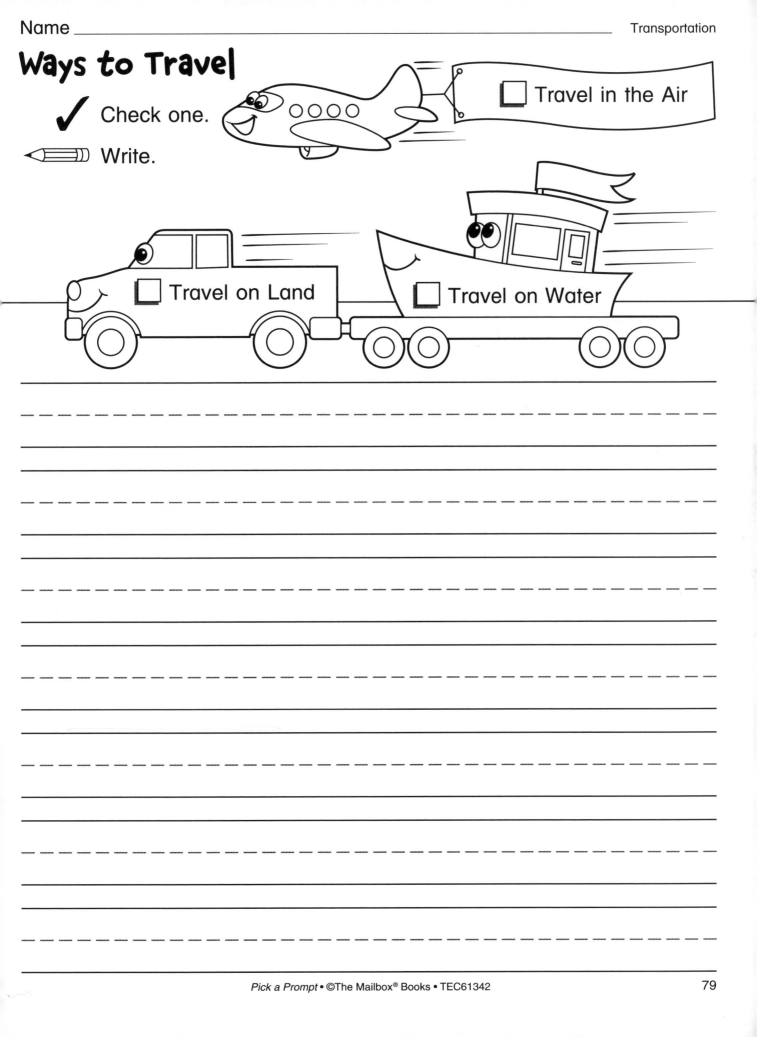

✓ Check one.

✏ Write.

☐ Travel in the Air

☐ Travel on Land

☐ Travel on Water

Name _____

A Zany Zoo

✂ Cut.

▭ Glue.

✏ Write.

_____
_____
_____
_____
_____
_____
_____
_____

| My Trip to the Zany Zoo | On a real trip to the zoo,.... | Let me tell you about the turtles! |